MW01616492

The Usher's Book of the Mass

by the editors of MODERN LITURGY

RESOURCE

Resource Publications, Inc.
San Jose, California
Printed in Canada

Editorial directors: Kenneth Guentert, Nick Wagner
Prepress manager: Elizabeth J. Asborno
Illustrations: Stan Bomgarden

Reprint Department
Resource Publications, Inc.
160 E. Virginia Street #290
San Jose, CA 95112-5876

Library of Congress Cataloging in Publication Data
The usher's book of the Mass / by the editors of Modern
    Liturgy.
        p.   cm.
    ISBN 0-9390-364-7 (pbk.)
    1. Catholic Church—Liturgy—Handbooks, manuals, etc.
    2. Church ushers—Handbooks, manuals, etc. I. Modern
    Liturgy.
    BX1972.U84   1996
    264'.0203—dc20   96-4891

Printed in Canada

00 99 98 97 96 | 5 4 3 2 1

Contents

TO MINISTRY COORDINATORS

In order to help ushers better understand their role, many parishes now refer to this group as "hospitality ministers." However, the original meaning of "usher" was both "doorman" and "officer of justice." These are not at all inappropriate understandings of this ministry. In addition, many ushers do not feel comfortable with the term "hospitality minister," and this book is intended to be comfortable.

Having said that, one of the most uncomfortable changes in this ministry for many ushers is the introduction of women into their ranks. In some places, parishioners believe they will see women priests before they see women ushers! Every parish community will have to deal with the issue of recruiting women to this ministry in their own time and in their own way. For the purposes of this book, we have presumed that women may be serving in the role of usher in your parish. There is certainly nothing that supports restricting women from this ministry, neither in canon law nor in the tradition of the liturgy.

The core of this book was originally written for altar servers. Many ushers (the men, anyway) began their liturgical ministry in the church as servers. But much has changed since many of us served at the altar. This book is not so much about how to be an usher (though there is some of that) but to answer questions about those changes and even to raise some challenges.

The Usher's Book of the Mass presents sophisticated liturgical information in clear language. That is to say it is concrete, colorful, and direct. It is also playful. But it has the utterly serious purpose of trying to give ushers some sense of "the holy"— especially as it relates to our worship.

The Usher's Book
of the Mass

HOLY

In this book, we'll often use the word "holy." This does not mean "good" or "nice" or "better than" or "like an angel." In Hebrew, the word *kodesh* means "holy" in the sense of "set aside" or "special." You are "holy" in that sense because you are an usher.

A HOLY PEOPLE

You are part of a "holy people." This does not mean you are better than people who do not go to your church or who do not believe in your God. It means you are part of a special community, one special to God, with special responsibilities to make the world a better place.

As an usher you are "holy" in another way. You have a special role to play— helping the members of the assembly feel comfortable. Your primary job is to be hospitable. In addition, you serve as a role model to the members of the assembly by actively participating in the Mass. As an usher you will also help with the collection. In addion, ushers usually come to church early to help the other ministers get ready and leave late in order to straighten things up when most people have gone.

There are other special (holy) roles too:

- The **assembly**, which sings, listens, and prays. The assembly has the most important role. Without people, there is no one to worship God.

- The **cross-bearer**, who carries the cross and leads the minister or people in procession. Sometimes an usher serves a cross-bearer in a pinch.

- The **torch-bearer**, who carries a candle in processions.

- The **lector**, who reads from the Bible.

- The **communion minister**, who helps to share the Body and Blood of Christ both with members of the assembly and with members of the community who are sick or otherwise unable to come to church.

- The **server** (or **acolyte**), who assists the presider.

- The **gift bearer**, who brings up the gifts at the presentation of gifts (formerlly called the "offertory") and sometimes prepares the altar table for the celebration.

- The **musician**, who helps the assembly pray with music.

- The **deacon**, who assists the presider, proclaims the Gospel, and sometimes preaches the homily.

- The **homilist**, who preaches and comments on the Scripture readings. (Often, the homilist and presider are the same person.)

- The **presider** is the priest who leads the liturgy and leads the assembly in prayer at Mass.

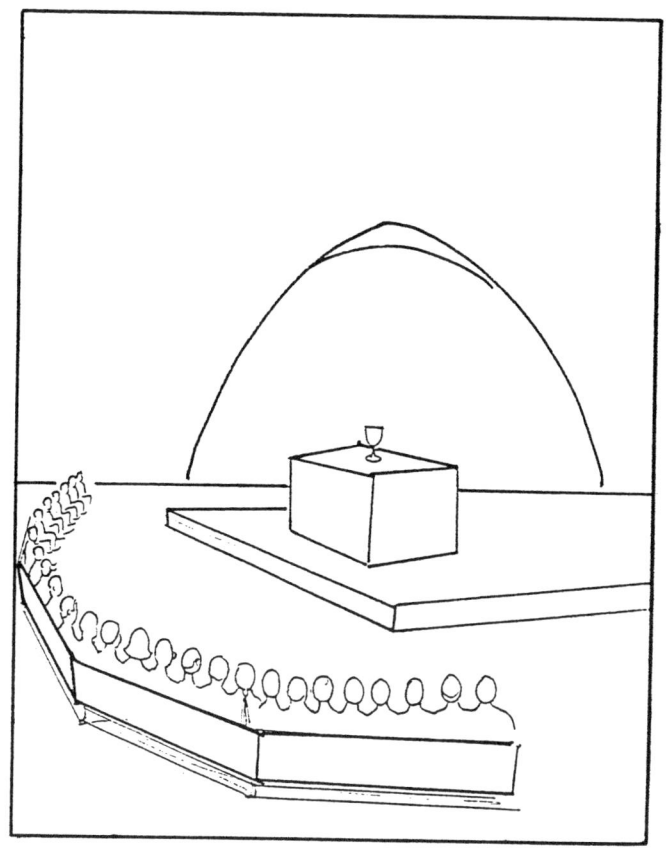

In addition, many other people behind the scenes make the Mass happen in a special way. There are **planners**, who plan the Sunday service weeks and sometimes months in advance; **artists**, who created the space you worship in and who decorate it from week to week with special banners, plants, and symbols; and **catechists**, who prepare candidates for the sacraments that might be celebrated at a Mass.

So every Sunday Mass is a special (holy) event.

HOLY TIMES

The entire Christian community gathers for worship at special times. The most special time for gathering is Sunday, which is the day that Jesus rose from the dead. So every Sunday, we remember Jesus' death and resurrection.

There are other days of the year when the entire assembly tries to gather for worship. In the United States, these days are:

- The Assumption of Mary (August 15)

- All Saints (November 1)

- The Immaculate Conception of Mary (December 8)

- Christmas (December 25)

- The Solemnity of Mary, the Mother of God (New Year's Day)

- The Ascension of Our Lord (a Thursday, forty days after Easter Sunday. In some places the Ascension is celebrated on the Seventh Sunday of Easter.)

These days are special to the United States and are called "holy days."

The *holiest time of the year* is a three-day feast called the Easter Triduum (after the Latin for "three-days"). Easter Triduum is one feast made up of three days beginning on Holy Thursday evening and ending on Easter Sunday evening.

Easter, in the eyes of the church, is not one day but fifty! It begins with the Triduum and lasts until Pentecost Sunday, seven weeks later.

The church is like the earth—it has its own seasons. Most of the year is called Ordinary Time because it's, well, ordinary, like most of the time. In between are the "extraordinary" times like Advent (four weeks), Christmas (several weeks), Lent (six weeks), and Easter (seven weeks). Each of these seasons has a different color and a different feeling about it—just as spring, summer, fall, and winter have their own moods and colors and special activities.

HOLY PLACE

Most assemblies set aside a special place to gather for worship. In olden times, people might have called such a place a "temple." We call it a "church," which is another word for "assembly."

Your church, no matter how different it is from churches in the next town, will have things in common with the temple where the Israelites worshiped God. For example:

The Tabernacle

This was God's home. In Moses' time, it was a large tent. No human, except for the high priest, even went into this tent—and he only went once a year. In our time, the tabernacle is a much smaller place where we keep the bread that has become the Body of Christ. It looks a little like a cupboard, but it is really a shelter for God. Years ago, the

17

tabernacle was part of the altar. Now it is often set away from the altar in a special devotional area.

The Altar

In Moses' time, the altar was very much like a barbecue. Really. Officially, it was called "an altar of holocaust," but that is fancy talk for a place where you cook meat. So why did the temple have a barbecue? You have to understand that for ancient people food was very important (that much should not be hard to understand). They believed that if they gave God some of their crop or flocks or herds—especially before they took anything for themselves—God would bless them with more food than they needed. So how do you give food to God? One way is to destroy the animal—by burning it—which is like sending it to another world. In later years, the priests kept these "holy sacrifices" for themselves and ate them. That was another way of getting the offering to God.

The altar in your church comes from that very same altar of holocaust. Of course, we don't burn anything there, but we still use the ancient language: "Lamb of God, who takes away the sin of the world...." At Passover, the angel of death "passed over" every house that had lamb's blood sprinkled on the doorway. The Israelites, therefore, would kill a lamb at Passover, burn it, and eat it as a way of remembering how they were saved from death. For us, the lamb of God is Christ and we remember how we were saved from death at every Mass.

Altars of holocaust were made of stone. Older altars in Catholic churches contain a stone with bone fragments from Christian martyrs. This is a concrete (pun intended) way of reminding you that this is indeed an altar of sacrifice.

The Table

In Moses' time, this was a piece of furniture that held the "bread of the Presence"—holy bread that was offered to God. In our churches, we place the bread on the altar—which is why the altar is sometimes also called "the table of the Lord" or an "altar table." It is really two pieces of furniture in one.

Lamp of God

In the Israelite temple, a lamp burned outside the tabernacle to show that God was inside his "house." In your church, you can find a lamp burning all the time to show that God is here too.

During the Easter season, look also for the **Easter candle**. It is there to remind you of Christ, the light of the world, and it is lit only when the assembly gathers for worship. That is because after resurrection, Christ lives in the people. If the people go out, the lamp goes out.

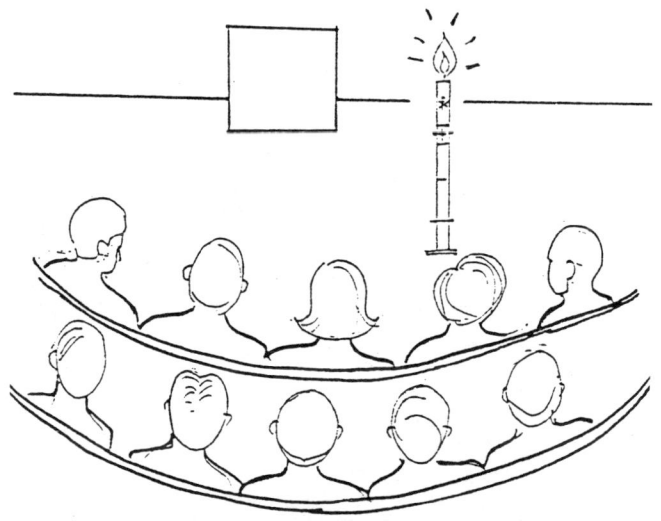

HOLY PLACE

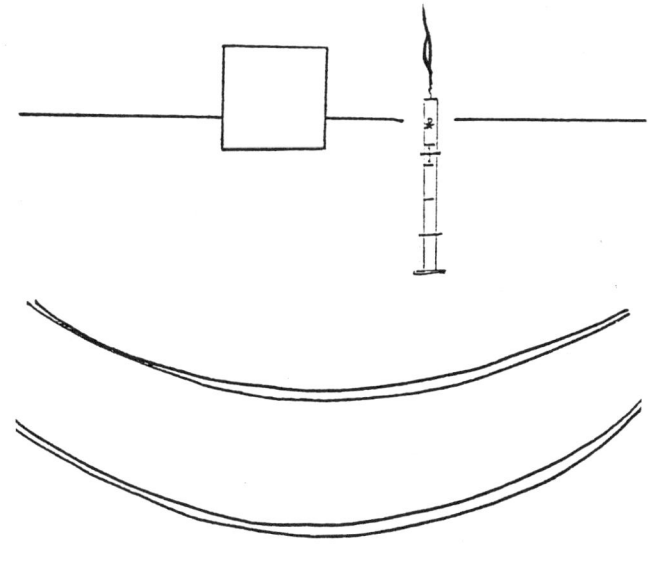

HOLY STORIES

Our Mass is like a two-part story. The first part is the Liturgy of the Word, and the second part is the Liturgy of the Eucharist. In the Liturgy of the Word, we tell stories. The stories come from three places. The first story or reading comes from the Hebrew Bible or other ancient texts. These are stories the Jewish people told for generations and generations before anyone wrote them down. They are the same stories Jesus often told in his ministry.

The second story or reading comes from the New Testament. These stories are usually letters that one of the apostles, like Paul or Peter, wrote to the first-century Christian communities.

The third and most important story or reading comes from the Gospel. "Gospel" is a Greek word that means "Good News." The Gospel is the story of Jesus' life, ministry, suffering, death, and resurrection. Jesus' story is the foundation of everything we believe and that is why it is the most important of the three.

As an usher, you have a very important role in helping the assembly get ready to hear these stories. When people come to church, often they are not thinking about coming to hear a story. They are thinking about finding a parking space, about whether their children will behave, about the grandparents coming over for brunch later, and dozens of other distractions. If, when they arrive, they see a friendly face—your face—welcoming them and helping them find a seat, it can help them settle more quickly and focus on the upcoming stories.

There will also be many strangers who come to church. Even the most outgoing stranger will have a little hesitation about whether he or she is really welcome. Think about the last time you visited another church. Did you immediately feel right at home? I bet not. Be on the lookout for strangers, and go out of your way to help them feel comfortable. Always remember to smile.

One more thing. Since these stories are so important, you want to do everything you can to minimize distractions while they are being proclaimed. So, even though it is important to help late-comers find seats, do so *between* the readings. Don't walk up and down the aisle during the readings. And, of course, you would never visit with friends or fellow ushers during the readings.

The second half of the Mass, the Liturgy of the Eucharist, comes from many stories about Jesus (and others). Here are two:

Story One

Jesus went up into the hills and sat down there. Great crowds came to him, bringing with them the lame, the blind, the mute, and many others, and they put them at his feet, and he healed them. Jesus called his disciples (students) together and said, "I am concerned about this crowd because they have been with me for three days and have had nothing to eat. I am afraid to send them away because they might get faint." His disciples said, "We're in the desert. Where can we get enough food to feed them?"

Jesus said, "How much bread do you have?"

They said, "Seven loaves, and a few fish."

Jesus told the crowds to sit down. *He took the seven loaves and the fish, and having given thanks, he broke them and gave them to his students, who gave them to the crowd.* And they all ate and were satisfied; and they took up seven baskets full of the broken pieces left over.

Those who ate were four thousand men, not counting women and children (Mt 15:29-38).

Story Two

Now as they were eating the Passover, Jesus *took bread, and blessed it, and broke it, and gave it* to his students and said, "Take, eat; this is my body." *And he took a cup, and when he had given thanks he gave it to them and they all drank from it.* And he said to them, "This is my blood of my covenant, which is poured out for many. Truly, I say to you, I shall not drink again of the fruit of the vine until that day when I drink it new in the kingdom of God" (Mk 14:22-25).

What do the two stories have in common? They each show Jesus *taking* bread, *blessing* it, *breaking* it, and *sharing* it with his friends.

How are the two stories different? The first is about bread and fish, and the second is about bread and wine.

Fortunately, we take our Mass from the second story; otherwise we might be eating bread and sardines on Sunday morning!

But the two stories are almost the same. What is important is taking up the food or drink, blessing God for giving us these good things, breaking the bread and pouring out the wine, and then sharing them with our friends.

Can you name the four important actions?

1. Taking up the bread and wine

2. Blessing God for the gifts

3. Breaking the bread, pouring out the wine

4. Sharing the bread and wine with friends

It is important to know the four actions because the Liturgy of the Eucharist really consists of the same four parts. The four parts have fancy names, but they are the same four actions.

1. Preparation of the Gifts (taking up bread and wine)

2. Eucharistic Prayer (blessing God)

3. Fraction Rite (breaking bread/pouring out wine)

4. Communion (sharing bread and wine)

Can you recognize these four parts in the Liturgy of the Eucharist?

1. Preparation of the Gifts

During this part of the Mass, which used to be called the "offertory," many things happen.

One of the first things that happens is you take up the collection. The collection is not simply a way to fund the ministries of the parish and pay the heat and light bill. It is a very important part of the Mass. The offering of money represents the lives of the members of the assembly. Most of us spend most of our days earning money. The way we spend our money tells the world what we think is important. In the early days of the church—and still today in some parts of the world—the poorer Christians did not have cash. So they gave food during the collection. The deacon would look over the food and select the best bread and the best wine that had been given to use for the Eucharist. Now, the money we give is used to buy the bread and wine we offer at Mass.

Some parishes use baskets or bowls that are passed back and forth between rows for the collection. Other parishes use baskets with long handles on them that are extended down the row by the usher. In either case, always be hospitable when passing the basket. Never hold the basket in front of an individual, "waiting" when it is clear that he or she does not intend to put anything in. Some people prefer to give in secret and do not contribute during the collection time. Also, although it is important not to dally, the collection should not look like an exercise by a military drill team. Be friendly and a little laid back. Imagine you are Jesus asking the disciples if they have any bread to share.

Many other things happen during the preparation of the gifts. The assembly sings; gift bearers bring the bread and wine (and other offerings) to the altar table; someone "sets the table" with the corporal (table cloth), the purificator (small towel), the Sacramentary (one of the holy books), the cup, and the basket or ciborium of bread; the presider prepares the bread and wine and says some prayers over them; the presider or deacon mixes some water with the wine; the presider says some prayers to himself; the presider washes his hands; the presider invites the assembly to pray.

These actions are all "preparation." That is why we call this part of the Mass "the preparation of the gifts."

Think of the preparation of the gifts as preparation for a fancy meal, Thanksgiving dinner perhaps. Obviously, your preparations for the meal are not the highlight of the day, but if you don't prepare the food and set the table, nobody eats. So it is important in this way.

2. Eucharistic Prayer

When Jesus took the bread in his hands, he said a Jewish prayer something like, "Blessed are You, O Lord, Our God, King of the Universe, who gave us the bread of life."

Our prayer is *much* longer and more complex, but it sill includes a long section blessing God for his wonderful gifts. In addition, you will hear:

- a retelling of the story (remember the four actions) by the presider and a response from the assembly that reminds us of how Jesus died, rose from the dead, and will return one day

- prayers for the living and the dead

- a "Great Amen" as the people's response (you included) to this long prayer

- the Our Father

- an exchange of peace

3. The Fraction Rite

In olden times, the Mass was called "The Breaking of the Bread." The part where this happens now is called the fraction rite ("fraction," which sounds like "fracture," means "breaking"). A good way for this to happen is for the presider to take a loaf of bread, perhaps baked by someone from the parish, and break it into little pieces that can be given to members of the assembly. This is a very strong reminder that each of us belongs to one body (loaf).

The pouring of the wine from one cup into other cups which can be shared by members of the assembly is much the same reminder. All God's people drink from the same cup.

The fraction rite is also a reminder that Jesus' body was "broken" for us and that his blood was "poured out" for us.

The fraction rite is also when we say the "Lamb of God" prayer.

4. Communion

This is when Christians share the consecrated bread and wine with each other. This is also a time when ushers may be a little too visible. In most parishes, the ushers will come forward during the Lamb of God and stand at the front pews ready to direct people to communion. Imagine for a moment that all the ushers in your parish forgot to come forward at that moment next Sunday. Would the people still be able to receive communion? Of course they would. They probably wouldn't even notice there were no ushers "helping" them. However, helping people to communion when they really don't need it would not be a problem if that was all there was to it. But moving to the front of the church during the Lamb of God (or during the Our Father, or during any other prayer or song) distracts people from the more important action of the liturgy. So if you must come forward to assist with the lines for communion, do so at a time when your movement will not be noticed, perhaps when the communion ministers come forward or perhaps during the sign of peace. But even better, if you are really not needed, go and sit with your family or some friends and receive communion with them.

Dismissal

After communion is over, Mass usually ends quickly. It is your job to hand out the bulletin and other flyers to the people as they leave. However, your more important job is to be a role model to the other members of the assembly. Therefore it is important for you to remain in the main worship space for the final song, all the way through to the last verse. Some people will leave before that, and they may need to pick up a bulletin off the tables, but they will see that you think Mass is important enough to stay through to the end.

HOLY FOODS

Bread

If the bread you see at Mass looks more like a cracker than bread, just remember the story of the first Passover. The Israelites ate "unleavened bread" because they were in a hurry to get away from the Egyptians. Normal bread, with leaven or yeast, takes an hour or two to rise. The Israelites had no time. Centuries later, Jesus and the apostles ate unleavened bread on the feast of the Passover as a way to remember the freeing of their ancestors from Egypt. Centuries after Jesus, we frequently use unleavened bread at our Mass—and that's a way of remembering Jesus who was remembering Moses.

If your church uses bread that looks and tastes like bread, enjoy. That is the way it is supposed to be. Remember: in olden times, bread was very nourishing and was sometimes all that people ate. Bread represents all food and means "life." If you share bread with your neighbors, that means you are willing to share your life with them. Sometimes, people still call wheat "the staff of life." If you look around, maybe you can find a picture of wheat somewhere in your church.

Wine

In Jesus' time, wine was an everyday drink. Like bread, it also represents all drink and all life. It is red (sometimes), like blood, and full of "spirits" that can make people lively (if they don't drink too much). On ceremonial occasions, Jewish people took a cup of wine and gave a special blessing to God.

> "Blessed are you, O Lord Our God,
>   Ruler of the Universe,
>   who gave us the fruit of the vine."

If you listen closely, you will hear the priest say something like this during the preparation of the gifts, and you, along with other members of the assembly, will say, "Blessed be God forever."

At Passover, Jews say this prayer four times and drink four cups of wine. Jesus did the same thing when he celebrated Passover, including the time we call the Last Supper. We do the same as a way of remembering Jesus who was remembering his ancestors.

Fish

What? You eat no fish at Mass. Look around. You might find a fish symbol somewhere in your church, maybe by the baptismal font. The fish is an ancient symbol of Christianity, probably because Jesus lived by a lake and ate a lot of fish. Also, the early Christians noticed that the letters of the Greek word for "fish" (IXTHUS) stood for "Jesus Christ, Son of God, Savior."

Why might you find a fish by the baptismal font? Because a fish cannot live outside of water. Neither can a Christian.

Water

You will find water at the Mass, too. Just like bread and wine, water represents life too. You can live a long time without food, but only a few days without water. Look for water at the baptismal font. That is the most important place. But you will also see water used at Mass. Can you say when? During the preparation of the gifts, the priest mixes a little water with the wine and later washes his hands with water.

Remember, though, that the most important water is in the baptismal font. If the baptismal font is at the door of your church, you can bless yourself with its water as you enter. If the presider or another minister sprinkles the assembly with water—as he will do on some special feasts—you can think of the life-giving water of the baptismal water. "Holy water" is really baptismal water.

42

TABLE SERVICE

The altar is also a table, and as a table it has dishes, linens, and candles. The most important item is the Cup.

The Cup

The cup (sometimes called a "chalice") is the most important part of our "table setting."

In the Middle East, where Jesus came from, drinking from a common cup was a very powerful symbol. It meant you were willing to shed your blood for those who drank with you. Soldiers drank from the same cup before they want into battle. Jesus and the apostles drank from the same cup on the night before Jesus died. That, by the way, was why Peter cut off the soldier's ear in the Garden of Gethsemane and why he felt so bad when he wound up denying Jesus three times. He had pledged to defend Jesus with his life—and he couldn't even admit he knew him!

The important thing about the cup is that we share it. Those who drink from the cup bind themselves to each other and to Jesus, the Messiah. That is why drinking from the cup is one way to receive communion.

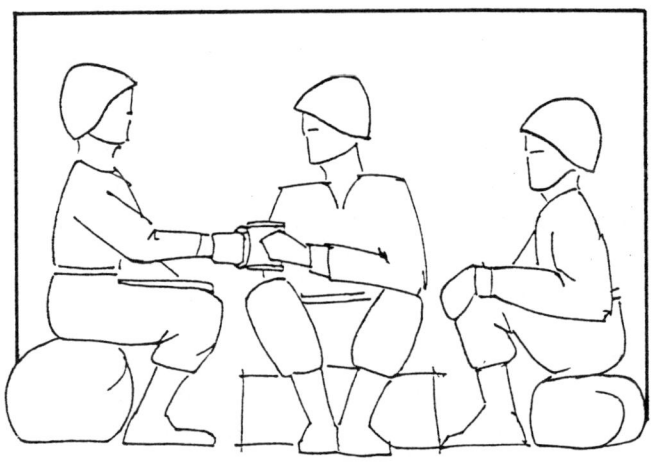

Breadplate

An old name for this is "paten". It holds the bread that will be broken up and shared.

Breadbaskets

These hold the small or broken pieces of bread that the communion ministers give to members of the assembly. Sometimes they are baskets. Sometimes they are ceramic or gold containers. Years ago we used a container called a "ciborium" that looked very much like the chalice.

Candles

The Mass is a ceremonial meal. Just as your family might do for Thanksgiving, we set out candles. It makes the meal more special (or holy).

Tablecloth

Ceremonial meals often have a tablecloth. You might see one of these too. If there is no large tablecloth, you can find a small square piece of cloth called a "corporal" that represents a tablecloth.

Purificator

The priest uses another piece of cloth for cleaning the cup. Think of the purificator as a small towel.

Cruets

These are small pitchers that hold the wine and the water.

Flagon

If the assembly is going to share the cup, the wine might be brought up at the preparation of the gifts in a larger container called a "flagon."

HOLY BOOKS

You should be able to identify three books.

1. *The Book of the Gospels.* This book
   contains the Gospel reading for all
   the Masses of the year. This book
   may be decorated with special
   material, depending on the season or
   feast. A lector may carry this book
   high about his or her head at the
   entrance procession and place it
   upon the altar. The presider or
   deacon reads from it at the Gospel.

2. *The Lectionary.* This book contains
   all the readings for all the Masses of
   the year. The lectors will read from
   this book.

3. *The Sacramentary.* This book
    contains all the other prayers and
    instructions for the Mass.

All of these books are special (holy). Treat them
with respect before, during, and after Mass.

HOLY FURNITURE

Do you have special furniture in your house, perhaps a dining-room table? In some families, the dining-room table is the most expensive piece of furniture in the house, chosen with care, dusted and polished frequently, and used only on very special occasions. The furniture in your church is like this. It has probably been specially designed just for your church. The artists who made this furniture loved working with the wood, the stone, and the metals that your parish chose for this furniture. The artists did their very best work for you. And they placed it in your church so that everything goes together. Be sure to honor this furniture and the work that went into it, especially these pieces.

The Altar Table

This is the largest piece of furniture and is the focus of attention during the Liturgy of the Eucharist.

The Ambo, Lectern, or Pulpit

The first part of the Mass, the Liturgy of the Word, is centered here. You'll see the lectors come to the ambo for the first two readings, the priest or deacon for the Gospel, and the preacher for the homily. Sometimes the cantor also leads the psalm from the ambo because it, too, is the Word of God.

The Chair

This is the large chair where the presider sits.

The Font

This is the basin or pool of water where new Christians are baptized. In some churches, by the doors, there are smaller fonts containing holy water which remind us of the water of baptism.

HOLY GARMENTS

One way to show that an event or a celebration is special is to wear special clothing. If you are a baseball player, you wear a uniform. If you are invited to a wedding, you put on your best duds. If you are graduating, you wear a gown that marks you as a graduate. The more special the occasion, the more special the clothes. Sometimes clothes are so special you wear them only at certain times. You don't wear your football helmet to a dance; you don't go fishing in a tuxedo.

The Mass is a special occasion that requires special clothing. The special clothing even has a special name: "vestments."

The important ones are:

- the **alb**, which many ministers, including altar servers, may wear

- the **stole**, a long garment the priest wears around the neck. The priest wears at least a small stole for all of the sacraments.

- the **chasuble**, a large garment that can be very dramatic and beautiful. The chasuble makes the priest's gestures and blessings easier for the assembly to see.

HOLY MOVEMENT

You can help make the Mass feel like a special moment—just by the way you move. You can also teach people how to behave.

Sitting

Sit with your head up, back straight, and feet on the ground.

Kneeling

Kneel with your back straight and your head up. Don't sit back on your heels. Don't kneel just on one knee when you are kneeling in the aisle, perhaps after the Lamb of God. Kneel on both knees.

Walking

Walk with your head up and back straight—and walk more slowly than normal.

Singing

Make sure you have a hymnal or songbook at your place. Use it when you're not busy with another task. Other people will notice and will feel more comfortable singing too.

Listening

Pay attention to the lectors when they read the Scripture. You may not think anybody can tell if you're listening, but believe me, we can. And we'll be more apt to listen too if you do. (Listen, though; don't read along in a missalette.)

Handshaking

One exception to the "move slowly" rule might be the sign of peace. Go ahead and greet people at your normal speed. Be sure to smile, and make sure your handshake is firm and friendly. And it's a nice touch if you go out of your way to greet your own family.

PROCESSIONAL ITEMS

The Cross

Sometimes you may act as cross-bearer, leading all the ministers and sometimes the entire assembly (on Passion Sunday, for example) in procession. You will put the cross in a prominent location. The cross is an essential element for Mass; sometimes there will be a large cross behind or above the altar, but increasingly the main cross is the one you carry in procession.

The Book of the Gospels

Often the lector or deacon will carry this in procession, holding it over his or her head so that the people can see it and realize how important is the Word of God. On reaching the sanctuary, the book-bearer places the book in a prominent position.

Candles

The acolyte or torchbearer will carry candles in the procession.

A procession is not . . .

. . . a race.

ORDER OF THE MASS

Gathering Rites

- Gathering Song and Procession
- Greetings from the Presider
- Kyrie (Lord, Have Mercy)
- Glory to God
- Opening Prayer

Liturgy of the Word

- First Reading (from Hebrew Scriptures or Acts of the Apostles)
- Psalm Response
- Second Reading (from the letters or the Book of Revelation)

- Gospel Acclamation
- Third Reading (from the Gospels)
- Homily
- Profession of Faith
- General Intercessions

Liturgy of the Eucharist (Preparation Rites)

- Setting the table
- Procession and song
- Prayers over the bread and wine
- Mingling of water and wine
- Prayer of the priest (said softly)
- Washing of hands
- Prayer over the Gifts

Liturgy of the Eucharist (Eucharistic Prayer)

- Preface
- Holy, Holy, Holy Lord
- Consecration and story
- Memorial Acclamation (remembering Christ's death, resurrection, and second coming)

- Anamnesis (remembering)

- Intercessions and commemorations

- Great Amen

Liturgy of the Eucharist (Communion Rite)

- Lord's Prayer

- Rite of Peace

- Fraction Rite (Breaking of Bread)

- Lamb of God

- Invitation to Communion

- Sharing of Eucharist and Communion Song

- Silent Prayer or Song of Thanksgiving

- Prayer after Communion

Concluding Rites

- Final Blessing

- Dismissal

- Recession of Ministers

- Closing Song (optional)